Hand on My Heart

Poems

by Anara Guard

New Wind Publishing

New Wind Publishing | Sacramento

Copyright © 2019 by Anara Guard

All rights reserved. No part of this book may be used or reproduced in any manner without written permission except in the case of brief quotations embodied in critical articles and reviews. For permissions, contact the publisher at info@newwindpublishing.com

Guard, Anara
Hand on My Heart: poems / by Anara Guard
p. cm.
Hand on My Heart/ Anara Guard -- 1st ed.
ISBN 978-1-929777-13-6
LCCN 2019914001
      I.   Title.
811'.54—dc22

Printed in the United States of America by
New Wind Publishing
5315 Spilman Avenue
Sacramento, California 95819
www.newwindpublishing.com

Printed in the United States of America

Cover design by Karen Phillips/PhillipsCovers.com
Logo design by Jim Hunt

Praise for *Hand on My Heart*

Hand on My Heart is a collection that dives into one's "own mysterious depths/the volcanic source revealed," as Anara writes in the poem, "Self-Examination." With great range, she explores in lovely language the "Weekly Communion" of trash day, of owls, of the gift of a Mason jar that gets reused again and again. Dip in and savor these poems, one at a time, then return for more sips of poetic nectar.

— Jan Haag, author of *Companion Spirit*

Praise for *The Sound of One Body: Stories*

These strong, haunting stories are like small wounds, nothing fatal, but nevertheless permanent; not scars but bruises won in battle, each one a glancing blow that leaves a distinct mark, and a memory of the pain we can inflict or endure when we're not even looking.

— Robert Goolrick, author of *A Reliable Wife*

These fine stories offer brief, knowing glimpses into lives in transition. Anara Guard is a writer to be read again and again.

— Bret Anthony Johnston, author of *Corpus Christi: Stories*

Praise for *Remedies for Hunger: Stories*

Reading these stories is like walking through the house next door, with its everyday miracles and betrayals, both familiar and unfamiliar at the same time. Guard's stories are a pleasure to read...powerful and memorable, and although not long, they require time for reflection. These stories are luscious food for thought.

— *Chicago Book Review*

Anara Guard has an eye for the offbeat detail, the peculiar utterance, lending her stories a realism that is not only magical but also quirky and funny. She conjures a kind of enchanted landscape whose perils are navigated by characters who must contend with the oddness of their reality. These darkly whimsical stories of misfits—a girl who doesn't know left from right, a mother who bleaches her children's eyebrows, a realtor showing a house to a bear—unfold in delightfully unexpected ways.

— Abby Bardi, author of *The Book of Fred*

These short stories are snapshots of urban life, intertwined with scenes from the country or the odd suburb...stories about children, con men, hippies, sweet fathers, and negligent mothers. Anara Guard picks out the secret jewels of the hardscrabble life where the domestic scene reveals the larger landscape. Her subject is the mystery of childhood, the certainty of death and the shining light somewhere in between with all its startling beauty.

— Lisa Page, Director of Creative Writing
George Washington University

*For DBH, as always,
and
for my sister in revelry*

Answers and Questions 1
All My Pretty Horses   3
Self-Examination   4
Yes, She Knew   5
Abandonment   7
The Bat Ray Cure   8
Mr I   9
Death after Dementia   10
>45   11

Laments 13
Hole in My Head   15
Regret   16
Heat Wave   17
I don't remember Thanksgivings past   18
Insomnia, Revealed   19
None for Me   20
Auntie Em's Lament   21

Praise and Petitions 23
Weekly Communion   25
Ice Fishing   26
At the Church of Winter   27
What Came from This   28
Owls   29
During the Service   30
Manmade Lake   31
The New Commandments   32
The Gift   33

Love, Maybe—and Love, Certainly 35
The Melt   37
Excuse Note   38
A True Story   39
Prophecy   40
Reconciliation   41
The Hedgehog's Map   42
The Lecturer   45
Robert Bly Reads His Poetry   46
Long Distance Love   47
Our Second Language   48
An Education   49
Illuminations   52

Answers and Questions

All My Pretty Horses

Let them canter before me, all my girlhood horses:
    Pinto, Percheron, Paint.
        Misty, Star, Appaloosa, Velvet,
            Black Beauty and Bucephalus,
                Pegasus, Flicka and Thunderbird.

Kings of the wind,
    I call on you now:
        brown and black and bay.

My friends, offer me your broad backs
    and something to cling to,
        reins or manes for my fingers to grip,
        and trot me to safety.

Lift me up, it is time to ride—
    bareback so that I may feel your heat.
        Let us fly into the dark, like all night mares,
        screaming into the wind.

I need to ride at full gallop,
    headlong, headstrong, forlorn,
        thundering to the childless horizon.

Self-Examination

With the help of a mirror and speculum
at last I am able to look within,
in to my own mysterious depths,
the volcanic source revealed.

I've always imagined lush colors there—
scarlet, violet, the passionate hues.
Indeed, the cervix is purple:
round and soft like a breast.

Each of us floated beyond it once
wrapped in the liquid uterus.
The universe pulsed, the cervix stretched—
we tumbled to the earth.

From the roomful of faces beyond my knees
women emerge. One by one,
they bend and peer with light in hand
to know my body as their own.

We smile to recognize the route,
the cycles and rhythms of our home.
Is it our own births we now recall
or those of our children, yet unborn?

Yes, She Knew

In answer to WB Yeats' poem, "Leda and the Swan,"
which asked
"Did she put on his knowledge with his power?"

Yes, she gained his power,
yes, she knew.

As he soared toward the open nest,
(wrapping her in his light white wings
as if she were his only child),
while he dived to the target's eye,
she saw the wild earth revealed:
distant, distinct, real.

They flew above forests
heaving with rain,
and she watched the flamingos dance
their naked pink seduction.
She saw the deserts,
scraped clean to the bone.

From her swaying, balanced cradle
she saw the acorn blossom into oak,
she knew what the white bull did,
what the shower of gold bought.

And she heard the swan's sole song,
not yet sung.
It sounded like temples falling,
like all women sighing together.

Up and over the world they rose
until it was a ball she once tossed high
from her father's garden into the air.
Blue, green, it whirled, and disappeared.

Abandonment

O children, unborn and unnamed –
my own, but alien, flesh.

How could I be free,
captured by your shrieks?
Would you think I desert you
when I put you to sleep?

What should I do
to halt your hungry cries
if you have sucked
these poor breasts dry?

You'd grow eager to explore.
Impatiently, you'd try to slip
away, you'd struggle terribly,
alive and warm in my fierce grip.

Little beasts, my children,
sweet monsters:
Wrapt in a raw, pink-pearl egg,
you undid me, demanding this:

my self for yours,
renunciation,
the sacrificial gift.

The Bat Ray Cure

She plunges an arm into the shallow pool
hoping to touch a bat ray
as it silently glides by.
But not with her left.
That one is cross-hatched with thin white scars
as if she has marked her achievements
or days imprisoned in solitary.
Such a sad measure, etched into her skin.
Use your left arm, my dear!
Baptize it in those briny waters
and brush the ray's velvety surface
with your inept fingers.
Release the sharp edge, the jagged point,
the need to prove your pain.
Let go your fears. We believe you.
The ray will allow your soft caress—
will you?

Mr I

For our date I choose
the blue gown with stars
and an open back.

Propped, swaddled,
and admonished to lie still,
I enter your embrace.

The slab beneath me warms,
I close my eyes. But
once inside, you sound the alarm.
Sirens wail, something batters
against my shell: clank, clank.
I am not permitted to respond.

You do all the work
while I remain motionless
focused on breath.

I want to imagine
that your attention will be a cure,
all of this effort—
the vibrations and din,
your jackhammering barrage—
will heal me,
a resonance therapy of some kind.

But afterwards,
all I'm given is an image
that maps my pain
and tells me what I already knew:
my body is failing,
sandblasted by time,
and you have already forgotten me.

Death after Dementia

Released from bonds we did not know,
Whose scars we saw, the stranglehold,
A rocky dam held back the flow
Of memories, what once was known.

Released from bonds we cannot know,
Held in a land we pray never to go.
Without a map, you wandered slow.
Did you hear our voices? Or your own?

Released from bonds, at last we know
A gentler grasp now has your hold.
The wind dies down, your mind is whole.

>45

What is greater than forty-five?

The stars in a smallest corner of the sky
Stars on the U.S. flag

Trombones in the big parade
and keys on a piano

Any mountain, anywhere, anytime
The Statue of Liberty's height
My height

Teeth in a shark's jaw
Bones in the human body
Eggs laid by a common toad
Days a child grows within the womb

Bottles of beer on the wall
Cards in a deck, even after we remove all the jokers

Colors in the big box of crayons
Native American nations

Body temperature
Boiling temperature
The lines on the 1040 tax form where you must reveal
your income tax *and* your payments made

Number of days the Montgomery bus boycott lasted
And months of the United Farm Workers grape boycott

Your zip code
Age of our republic
The call numbers of every public radio station

The price of freedom
The cost of justice

The Dewey Decimal numbers for all books on history, literature, science, technology, psychology, philosophy, politics, religion, language, journalism, travel, and art.

What is greater than 45?

Whether measured in length,
   width,
      height,
         depth,
            time,
               temperature,
                  frequency,
                     price,
                        span,
                           count,
                              cost,
                                 distance,
                                    breadth,
                                       duration,
                                          or significance,

what is greater than 45?

                        We are.

Laments

Hole in My Head

I have a hole in my head
and a word belongs in it.
The hole forms the exact shape
of that word I cannot remember.
You know what I mean,
what I mean to mean,
the word that describes that thing.
Oh, I can almost recall it!
I run my mind round the edge of the hole
like probing a missing tooth with my tongue.
It starts with a T. Or maybe a P
and it's about three syllables long.
I remember my sister saying it once
while we fought over who tore her paper doll.
Our room was painted pink.
The wallpaper peeled in one corner,
revealing dingy yellow beneath.
We had wooden bunkbeds. My pillow was flat
and smelled like foam rubber.
Her paper doll had brown curls and a smile.
Even with her amputated arm, she looked carefree.
Where is that word?
I need it to fill a hole
in my heart.

Regret

I have waited too long to prune
and my roses have grown tangled
and straggly. They resist
all efforts to tame them now.
I should have done this long ago,
should have fed them better, trimmed more often,
made more effort to coax them into graceful forms.
But the canes sprawl every which way, leaning
into each other, too leggy, hooked together,
unwilling to stand alone.
Pale blossoms nod limply at the top,
leaving the middle a thicket of thorns
that wound me as I try—too late!—
to shape these stubborn green branches.

Heat Wave

It's another hot evening and the city swelters,
fat, beached, and breathing
to the lonely rhythm of the basketball
bouncing down the street.

The ice cream vendor pedals slowly,
searching each face for thirst.
He jingles his bells and his money,
promises a melting relief.

In the middle of the intersection
a car stalls, its hood lifts in surrender.
The driver bends over the engine,
his gritty sweat feeding it like an IV drip.

Soon, he will abandon this effort,
head to the dark igloo of a bar,
sit shoulder to shoulder
with his anonymous brothers,

waiting for the sun to drop
like a bright coin into a slot machine.
The city holds its breath in hope
of winning something, anything, cool.

I don't remember Thanksgivings past

I don't recall giving thanks:
no prayers at our home, no offered grace.
We scraped by, as abrasive as the green pad
floating on top of greasy dishwater.

I don't remember the canned cranberries,
dead turkey, that horrible tablecloth:
red and green convolutions
in an endless blinding pattern.

I don't remember arguing over the knives—
never sharp enough.
Not as sharp as my mother's tongue.

I don't remember my brother, hunched in his chair
hoping to be overlooked this time—
nor the looks on our faces,
barely muted by candlelight.

I don't recall how the wine spilled,
how I clenched my teeth as it slowly soaked in.
I don't remember my sister leaving,
yelling as she thundered up the stairs:
she was running away, she would never come down.
She always kept her suitcase packed
and her nine dollars in savings ready.

I don't remember saving anything.
I left it there, gelid as turkey fat
on the white platter that never washed clean.

Emptied of memory,
I devour this year's feast.

Insomnia, Revealed

The restless night has laid claim to me
once again. Unable to stop thinking,
I stretch and moan, attack my pillows,
thrash with the blankets and sheets.
Sleep is an elusive imp, just beyond reach,
like a bird outside the window, tormenting the cat.

I should get up, make tea, surrender
to the impossibility of sleep.
But the moment this thought emerges,
my limbs are drugged with lassitude.
There is nothing I want less now than to move,
to become vertical or animated.

The way to find sleep is to reject it
like a mirage in peripheral vision
that cannot tolerate being seen.
Like the lover who spurns you
until you turn your back
and then he wants only you.

None for Me

After the crash, you must have scattered
Over yards and acres, into the next county or
Even somehow across state lines
Because there is your ponytail
Tumbling down the back of a stranger.
Your eyebrow cocks on an unfamiliar face,
And the shape of your shoulders is silhouetted
In each lit window I pass by at night.
How did all those people end up with a piece of you
And me, left with none?

Auntie Em's Lament

They say, after you've seen a twister
you're not the same. It mixed her
up, all right. Sometimes I miss her,
the girl she was, daughter of my sister.
Now the hens are scattered, my hands a-blistered,
fences down, but she just clicks her
heels together once, twice, and then quicker,
watching the clouds as if they'll lift her.
If only she had come with us into the shelter.
Where did she go? What does she wish for?
She's planting poppies out in the pasture!
Says that the scarecrow speaks in a whisper.
But if I go into the fields with her,
he's dumb as a post. Oh, I could list her
faults all day. I'm always chasing after
her to milk the cow, to sweep up faster.
She stares at the broom. When I ask her,
What's wrong, Dorothy? What is the matter?
she says *I didn't mean to come back here.*
Lord help me, sometimes I want to smack her.
How many times do I have to tell her
there are no flying monkeys and if there were,
not in Kansas, that's for sure.
She has a figure now, makes her look older.
The hired hands watch her, growing bolder,
drawling that they're feeling hotter.
I snap, *Act like she's your own daughter!*
But all I get are smirks and laughter.

I tell her, *Sit. Shell peas. No chatter.*
She takes the swing, I take the rocker,
then she starts talking and I can't stop her
from telling a tall tale about that twister:
Her ruby shoes. She talked with witches.
In an emerald city, she met a wizard.
I say, *Dorothy, you're just plain wicked
To tell such lies*. Her face is twisted
and she keeps on chanting,
she says it like a poem:
*There's no place like it,
no place like home.*

Praise and Petitions

Weekly Communion

We rise early on Tuesdays,
awakened by the rhythmic beeping of clock
and trash trucks, reversing toward us.
Across the sodden grass we pad, barefoot
or in soft slippers that shush over the driveway,
bearing our bins of glass—green, brown and clear.
Bottles with the taste of wine still lingering,
and shiny cans with no redemption.
At the altar of the curb, we offer our excesses,
hoping to be forgiven: reduce, recycle, reuse.
We mean, of course, ourselves,
bodies thick from lack of use.
We mean our hearts, heavy
with all that we forget.
Emptyhanded, we return to our doorsteps,
and the sprinklers anoint us,
whispering, "Bless, bless, bless."

Ice Fishing

After Mary miscarried,
she bent over the bowl
as if sick, or deep in prayer.
Her delicate fingers scrabbled
among the clotted strands
like a blind woman hunting eels.
Each viscous handful
dissolved before her eyes,
the ends of her hair
trailed in the murky water.

She begged for a small piece,
a pulse, a pearl to remain
when everything was gone.
When she looked up,
I knew she was drowning.

Later that spring, the lake ice
gave way too soon,
rotting from the bottom up.
Within their shacks,
the fishermen gasped
as the milky white floor decayed.
The cold holes they had drilled and watched
now gaped wide as a whale's maw,
swallowing shanties, trucks, all.

Mary and I watched the divers
raise six bodies into the soft air.
We blessed them
from where we stood on shore
before the earth had its chance
to bring them home.

At the Church of Winter

In January's deepest night
we dream of peaches
and weep when the clock wakes us.

Seagulls slow,
the frozen air too dense
for their wings to slice through,
their bodies heavy with chill.

At the bus stop, no one speaks.
We huddle like bison
in our shaggy robes,
withdrawing from the wind.
Skin shrinks against cold clothes,
bones contract in flesh,
eyeballs recoil from icy lids.

And deep within our coats, we bow,
sending foggy breath into our own hearts
praying for warm air,
wincing as we promise,
this time, not to forget
the blessings of July.

What Came from This

for Alan

"An odd sort of god comes out of this…"

Out of all this came an odd sort of god,
a cupid whose arrows were wrested away.
Nameless, sexless, you entered unknown
into pale flesh she did not show me.
I waited under the sheet, turgid, patient,
curiosity dulled by desire.
Your sound was lost in an ocean of moans,
your moment unnoticed by the movement and sweat.
We thought we were vigilant,
we crossed our fingers, but you entered,
smaller than a thumbprint,
and later emerged: pink familiar alien, sucked
into a whirlpool, vacuumed out
of this world and into the next.

I pray, but it is not quite forgiveness
that I ask for in the separate chambers of my heart:
it is understanding. Let me know
the name of stubborn persistence,
of the traveler who returns to me, small god,
like a lost bird, roosting in the face of the wind.
Unwelcomed, I want you just the same.

Owls

That afternoon when the owls flew,
you dropped to your knees,
breath caught in your throat.
Two birds burst from a bush, their startled wings
spread wide, eyes tight in the sun,
white bellies flashing in flight and you—
the skeptical one, wise as all
young philosophers are, confident in
rational discourse, matters of the mind—
you flung both hands up to God.
Your strong arms formed hosanna
when your lips would not.
Your knees bent without will,
thoughtless and sure of themselves,
seeking solid ground.
Epiphany of owl emerging: two great ghosts
whose wings beat the air
that heaved into your open mouth.
All language fled when the birds took flight.
Your heart swelled and seized the reins,
forcing you to pray,
seeking the meaning of white underwings,
of owls awakened in mid-afternoon.

During the Service

A breath of air stirs the pages of my hymnal
And I forget to listen to the minister's words.
Someone coughs behind me,
Sunlight illuminates a window,
One arm stretches overhead, belonging to a restless
    boy.

The young girl in the next pew
Strokes her own braid over and over
As if it is a tender pet
In need of comforting.

All around me, parishioners take solace
In their own ways, gazing at the ceiling
Or gently snoring or lost in thought.

This is how we pray.

Manmade Lake

Crossing the Texas plain in September,
in the back of a Ford with my sister and folks,
windows wide open to catch the hot breezes
that whistle like freight trains from the horizon,
I hear Daddy murmur to Momma,
"Soon, all this will be underwater."

My sister and I are astonished to silence:
the sun-bleached sky gives no sign of moisture.
A dragonfly shimmers, or is it a minnow?
That buzzard, who floats without any tether,
might be a seagull, searching for trash.

And those cattle—they'll drown, their brown eyes like
    bubbles,
panicked and rolling around and around.
These scrawny trees will be waving like seaweed
and the tumbleweeds turn into prickly blowfish.

Will Noah's flood reach into Texas,
the day of reckoning here at last (thank you Jesus)
and our parents again keeping it from us?

Now, everything opens to change:
deserts can be oceans and rivers run dry,
valleys slice through the unsteady earth.

We whisper together in the back seat,
urging the old Ford to flee toward home.
Lord, none but you can save us.
Your yellow eye watches.
We sweat as we pray,
please, please, don't send the rains.

The New Commandments

In the old days, rules were handed down:
adamant and faulty, carved into stone.
Now, God gives us simple directions
abbreviated onto small black keys.
These are our new commandments:
Function. Sleep. Save.
We press *Help* instead of praying.
God leaves it to us to choose: *Control?* or *Escape?*
If we can't do one, we try the other.
There is a command to be *Bold* and one to *End,*
Another to *Pause,* keep your fingers still.
God prompts us to *Delete* our errors,
Leaving only the white space of forgiveness.
Enter, God tells us. And we do.

The Gift

John Mason it was, who left us this gift:
a cup, a vase, a clear sarcophagus
for dragonflies or the smooth stones
we pluck from the beach. We may fill it with flowers.
The daisies hang their heavy heads
over the sides, bending down
to peer through the glass at their own spindly stems.

When we drink sweet tea straight from the jar
we remember to savor this moment,
to thank one another kindly,
to sit down while we sip.

Piccadilly, peaches, tomatoes, succotash:
this seal is meant to be broken.
Release the aroma of summer fruit,
the memories of picking, peeling, pickling,
the hot water bath in a steamy kitchen.

We preserve the jam and we save the jars,
using them again and again,
cycling through the years and the seasons,
boxes of jars lining the cellar shelves
in our grandmother's house
where we long to return.

Let us praise this humble flask which contains
   what we seek:
clarity and preservation.
For it is meant to be filled,
not halfway, but all the way,
to the brim,
to the seal,
to the lip we kiss with our own.

Love, Maybe—
and Love, Certainly

The Melt

Wet fun we had
Playing at battle
Pelting each other with our mock catapults.

We sweated too,
Scraping down to black pavement,
The harsh sounds of winter.

Now you gasp
Like cold slush down your collar:
Ambushed by my departure.

Why so surprised, love?
Surely you knew this could not last.
We were spring snow.

Excuse Note

Please excuse our tardiness today.
Our mother overslept, so we did too.
She didn't wake us up, like she should
and when she opened the front door
in her bathrobe and socks,
she said a bad word at the milk jug.
Its paper cap was lifted up,
a frozen cylinder of pale ice rose
out of the mouth of the cracked bottle.
My little brother laughed: it looked like a push-up!
that ice cream treat we sometimes got
from the drugstore at the corner.
We were disturbed, my sisters and me,
at how the ice had thrust itself upwards,
its queer paper cap askew.
Mom cursed the milkman, why
didn't he ring the bell when he left the bottle
on such a frigid morning?
But we knew that all this was her fault:
the thrust,
the ice,
the broken glass,
our tardiness today.

A True Story

Honey, we've hit the skids like the giraffe
    who fell
while fornicating.
    He slid,
his great legs stretched apart like
    a ladder.
Further and still further all four legs
    split.
A ton and a half of giraffe on the grass,
    stretched
the wrong way, sprung at the sockets,
    collapsed.
He lay with his long limbs all
    astraddle,
His spotted head drooped and his spirit
    dropped.
His tall harem two-stepped to tempt
    him,
swayed one behind the other, nudged his nose:
    get up.
But love sprawled on the ground,
    belly-flopped.
Nothing could rouse him, the weight on his
    heart,
like yours, like mine, more than we can
    bear.

Prophecy

The seer told me: He has dark matter in his soul.
Your love will not be reflected.
It will neither refract nor bend.
He will absorb every molecule you offer
and show no good effect.
You will know his presence
through the pull of his gravity, weighing you down.
He will give you a ring of lead, will feed you salt
and spread charcoal on your tongue.
His voice will penetrate through walls and beneath
    doors
so that you are never alone, not even in your dreams.

Reconciliation

You, who blocks my way—
    the bump in the road,
        snarl in my hair,
            the stutter, limp,
                stone in my shoe.

The stumble, the hobble, the turnstile—
    the crumbs in the sheet,
        grit in my eye,
            lump in my throat,
                my club foot.

You, who impedes me—
    stalls,
        brakes me,
            radio static,
                muscle cramp.

You—the rim,
    the rail,
        the holding edge,
           the hem, the belt,
                the safety strap.

Sunshade, sieve, net.
    My trigger lock.
        The filter, reins,
            the parachute creating drag—
                slowing my fall.

You, who catches me—
    cushions,
        the hand on my heart—
            the full stop—
                there.

The Hedgehog's Map

After months away at school and a trip overseas, you expect your son to be changed: taller perhaps, thinner, standing straighter. Or maybe he will be sloppy and unkempt. But he has shaved and his clothes, although not ironed, don't appear have been slept in. Unlike many nineteen-year-olds, he is still un-pierced and free of tattoos, and he grins at your obvious relief.

Wrap your arms around him and feel how solid he has become. That teenaged boniness that always reminded you of a gawky bird—shoulder blades and vertebrae sticking out every which way—is gone. In its place are muscle and flesh with a sense of structure beneath them.

His hair no longer tickles you because he is so tall, and has been to the barber that very morning. No more wisps hanging over his collar. He sports a military-style brush cut: short on top, almost nonexistent on the sides.

He looks younger with his hair so short, far too vulnerable to have such a raw recruit appearance. You wince to see how much of his tender skin is revealed and the shape of his skull, visible beneath his thin hair.

"Hedgehog," he declares happily. "That's what they call this haircut in Russian: *yozhik*." You reach up and rub the fuzz on his skull: softer than any hedgehog, more like a teddy bear for a young baby, the kind with silky fur and flappy limbs.

Then, already moving away from your embrace, he turns his head, and you see at the base of his skull, just above his neck, the birthmark.

Once, it was burgundy-red and nestled just where your hand supported his newborn head, when his neck muscles were still weak and undeveloped. The doctors were unconcerned: it will disappear on its own, they said.

They were wrong.

The mark faded but remained, an irregular map of an unnamed place. When he slipped into milky sleep, you traced its contours with the tip of your littlest finger. You dreamt this was the shape of a fairytale country from which he came. You imagined that, once upon a time, his entire body was that singular shade of rose-pink, and before he was born, the color drained away until all that remained was this little dreg at the back of his head, where he would never see it.

Like coral, the mark faintly glows through his clipped hair. Staring at it now in the sunshine of a new day, you wonder how you could possibly have forgotten it. How can you be startled now by a sight once so familiar you could have traced it in your sleep? You have been careless, neglectful; you buried a precious treasure and failed to mark its location. Now you stand, shovel in hand, helplessly gazing at a landscape with no signposts.

He turns again and looks at you intently. In his eyes, green flecked with brown, you see the loving gaze of a full-belly infant, the tempestuous challenge of a toddler on the verge of a tantrum, the wary plea of a first-day kindergartener, triumph of knowing how to read, glee of playing a joke on you, the dismissive flick of the adolescent's contempt, an unflinching assessment of your gray hairs, the fond acknowledgment of your tears.

He sees so much. But not the birthmark at the base of his skull. That sight is for you alone, reminder of a land that you have left far behind.

The Lecturer

Years of lectures have not quelled your fright;
from the thirtieth row, I see every tremor.
You stutter, but still, your vibrant tone,
as if played across a taut and quivering drum,
resonates through me, echoes and returns.

Your words roll forth, wrought more firmly now,
intense, fervent, seeking to appeal.
When the curtain drops, the thunder dies,
the buzzing crowd slowly files outside.
And still I tremble, filled with tenderness
for the courage of the solo human voice.

I would like to lay my lips on yours,
to feel the force that forms the words you speak.
The moth longs to flutter about the flame
or knock her senses out against the glass.
Her blinding efforts bring her burnt wings
and a brief memory of light, intensely seen.

Robert Bly Reads His Poetry

His hands form symbols as he speaks,
in choreographed motion,
suggesting Buddha, a Bali dancer,
and the language of the deaf.
Old hands, familiar with these words and voice
and this scruffy white hair
through which they tickle and search
between poems, uprooting
the work of the careless comb.
His voice rumbles of salt,
sulphur and lead,
and the longing of the fixed planets
for our fluctuating minds.
Each thing has movement, if it can.
and as he speaks, a feather
drifts into the spotlight,
floating slowly above his head,

Long Distance Love

The miles draw taut over the telephone line.
When I close my eyes to feel your breath in my ear,
I see the quiet land, sprawling in sleep between us.
I want to run my hands over the earth's surface
to feel the smooth curve of your skin,
play my fingers down ribs and valleys,
slide down hills of hips and knees, lick across
salt flats, see your face reflected
in each gleaming lake. Your silver hair streams
down mountain slopes; I kiss each cool strand.
The wind rustles your voice through the trees,
whispering under the blanket of night.

Our Second Language

Lying with my head on my lover's lap
I know how simple pleasure can be
And the pleasure of simplicity.
The complexities of the day distill
Themselves into moments pure, physical, rich:
We ate strawberries for breakfast.
Pizza later. We braided our hair,
Stroked small patches of skin
For long periods of time,
Wrote in pencil, noticed the sun on clouds.
Let's dream in Poetry
As if it were our second language,
The one we learn right after Touch.

An Education

You think, before the baby is born, that you will raise him
or her
without regard to gender.
Look how prepared you are,
with hand-me-down clothes dyed purple
to avoid pink or blue, and
a few picture books that you'll read aloud right away.
And with love.

It's a boy! And he arrives already knowing how to make
the universal "brrr..." sound of a motor with his baby lips
and he vibrates with joy at every truck he sees.
Now your education begins...
When the nextdoor neighbors build a new garage,
your toddler will not
be persuaded away from the window
although he can barely stand up
and must cling to the sill like a drunk.
He will insist on watching the cement mixer rotate
and the carpenters swing their hammers.
On each walk, you will have to stop the stroller wherever men
and equipment are at work:
digging out and chewing up a tree stump
or raising beams for a new building
or filling potholes in the street.

You will buy picture books full of trucks so you can learn
the differences between backhoe
and bulldozer, jackhammer and pile-driver.
Be sure to mark well which screwdriver is the Phillips
and which the straight
or your son will shake his head at you,

disappointed that you know
so very, very little about tools.
A winch and a wrench are not the same—
nor are a stegosaurus and a triceratops,
for dinosaurs will be the next area of interest
and you'll have some catching up to do.
The brontosaurus you grew up with never existed;
you need to know Allosaurus and Diplodocus,
not to be confused with the biggest-of-all Brachiosaurus!

Your next baby will be another boy
so you can take lessons in observing
how they wrestle and shove, climb trees, torment each other.
Ban toy guns from the house; they'll shoot anyway,
aiming at each other with forks, wooden spoons, chopsticks.
"Pow, pow!" a pistol fires.
"Pweeooh, pweeooh," answers the ray gun.

Did you not anticipate how fascinating it will be
to use a magnifying glass to make dry grass catch fire?
Has it never occurred to you that, if a boy pretends
to climb a mountain
by tying a rope
to the bookshelf
at the top
of the stairs,
he can pull the entire bookcase over, sending an avalanche
of books down the stairs
and terrifying everyone in the house?

Hang tight! There is much more to come:
Lego bricks and train tracks.
Shinguards and mouthguards.
Matchbox cars,
Magic the Gathering cards,
Dungeons and Dragons.
And then, computer programming.
They will seem nearly lost to you then,
deep within a maze of inscrutable symbols and arcane
commands. And. Or. Not.

You must discover tools to help you find a way to them,
Perhaps some bit of hardware or steel,
but for now,
here at the beginning,
the only path you know is to follow the thread of story,
and keep reading aloud
word after word of love.

Illuminations

Tonight, as I fly to you,
I hover at the window, peering down
over the dark land.
The moon is full,
it gleams on each watery surface below:
ponds, river, lakes lit silver
and when we pass, dims to black.
Like the magical hands in the fairy tale,
lighting her way down the corridor,
telling Beauty: there is no turning back;
like a necklace of fireflies
slowly winking on, then off,
each signaling the next to glow;
like a beacon pulsing its steady welcome
or the signalmen on the ground,
guiding the big bird home,
each light shines:
this way, this way to love.

Acknowledgments

Grateful acknowledgment is made to the editors of the following publications in which these poems or earlier versions of them have originally appeared:

"Abandonment" in *The Wild Word*, 2017

"Auntie Em's Lament" at *VerseWrights.com*, 2016

"Illuminations" in *Late Peaches: Poems by Sacramento Poets*, 2012, and at *VerseWrights.com*, 2016

"Manmade Lake" at *VerseWrights.com*, 2016

"Reconciliation" at *VerseWrights.com*, 2016

"Regret" in *The Wild Word*, 2017

"Robert Bly Reads His Poetry" in *HIKA*, 1977

"The Church of Winter" in *Convergence*, 2012

"The Gift" in *Sirsee*, 2017

"What Came from This" at *VerseWrights.com*, 2016

"Yes, She Knew" (as "Leda") in *HIKA*, 1975, and at *VerseWrights.com*, 2016

About the Author

Anara Guard grew up in the Midwest, lived in New England, and now resides in California. She has attended writing workshops at Urban Gateways, Columbia College, Bread Loaf Writers Workshop and Squaw Valley Community of Writers. Improbably, she has won both the John Crowe Ransom Poetry Prize from Kenyon College and the third-place Jack Kerouac Poetry Prize in Davis, California.

Anara has a B.A. in English, an M.S. in library and information science, and a certificate in maternal and child health.

In addition to poetry, Anara writes fiction and creative non-fiction. She is the author of the short story collections, *Remedies for Hunger* and *The Sound of One Body*, and four children's picture books.

Follow her at www.anaraguard.com or www.facebook.com/AnaraGuardAuthor/

About New Wind Publishing

New Wind Publishing is a small independent press located in Sacramento, California.

We believe in the craft of writing, the importance of books, and the ability of the written word to express truth, convey beauty, and change lives. We work closely and collaboratively with each writer through the stages of bringing a book to life.

If you have enjoyed this book, you may also enjoy *Red Thread Through a Rusty Needle,* poems by Gay Guard-Chamberlin (ISBN 978-1-929777-12-9). Gay and Anara perform their poetry together as "Sibling Revelry."

Visit www.NewWindPublishing.com to learn more, or request any of our books from your favorite local bookstore.

www.ingramcontent.com/pod-product-compliance
Lightning Source LLC
Chambersburg PA
CBHW020131130526
44591CB00032B/643